❊FOR❊

～ T H E ～
12 CATS *of*
CHRISTMAS

Story by
WENDY DARLING

Song by
EVELYN LOEB

Illustrations by
JAN PANICO

PETER PAUPER PRESS, INC.
WHITE PLAINS, NEW YORK

Story concept by S. M. Skolnick
Book design by Mullen & Katz

*Thanks to Marc Anello for
providing background material.*

Copyright ©1997
Peter Pauper Press, Inc.
202 Mamaroneck Avenue
White Plains, NY 10601
All rights reserved
ISBN 0-88088-063-5
Printed in China
7 6 5 4 3 2 1

ats
and Christmas have always
gone hand-in-hand or paw-
in-paw, if you will, in my life.
Rudolpha, my Grandma's
tabby, was unusually adept at
swatting ornaments (but
never breaking even one) that
hung from her richly decorated tree. Rudolpha's long

flowing coat added to the
apparent motion of her body
as she targeted a particularly
shiny globe suspended from
a low branch. Sometimes
I imagined I could see the
very ornament that she was
spying on reflected in her
hazel-colored eyes.

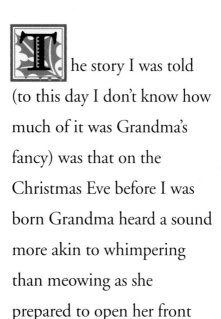

he story I was told (to this day I don't know how much of it was Grandma's fancy) was that on the Christmas Eve before I was born Grandma heard a sound more akin to whimpering than meowing as she prepared to open her front door. Wedged (I know this part is not true) between a milk can and a stone wall

was a "tiny shrivel of a thing with a puckery pink nose that was almost red, so I named her Rudolpha." Grandma went on to say that "Rudolpha's nose was so bright that she could have guided Santa's sleigh. Well at least she could have made a good tangle of Mrs. Claus' knitting yarn." Grandma brought the kitten inside, kept her warm and fed, and adopted her there and then. She said with a sly smile that she always knew my age because it was just about the same (give or take a few weeks) as Rudolpha's.

One year I was delivered to Grandma's house for an extended sleep-over several days before my family would return to join us on Christmas Eve.

Sitting in the bay window, unperturbed and appearing rather self satisfied as always, was Rudolpha.

The sight of that cat in the window reassured me that I was arriving at the right place, and wasn't accidentally being left with someone else's granny.

There were hugs and kisses all around.

My dad gave me a big squeeze and a kiss on the cheek. My mom took the opportunity of our parting to remind me of what seemed like an endless stream of "don'ts and don't forgets," like don't forget to brush your teeth, and wash your hands, and say please, and thank you, and don't go sledding down Northfield

Hill, and don't stretch across the table if you want the salt and pepper but say "could you please pass the ....," and on and on. She was equally careful to give Grandma (her very own mother) a list of don't let Wendy do this, and make sure Wendy does that, and don't keep her up late, and don't let her watch trash on the TV, etc. Just then Grandma said with mock exasperation (to her very own daughter), "It's a miracle that I raised you, your sister and your brothers without a set of instructions." Mom got the hint, gave Grandma another big kiss, and she and Dad were out the door and on their way home, not meant to return until Christmas Eve.

Finally it was just us three girls—Grandma,

Rudolpha, and me. The cat had come out of the bay and was cavorting the way only she could. Grandma began to place under the tree the presents that Mom and Dad had delivered with me. Rudolpha began to circle the brightly wrapped boxes, slapping at the ribbon, rolling herself underneath the branches, and totally enjoying her newly discovered love objects.

"Wendy dear," said Granny, "let's bake cookies." We sprinkled flour on the board, rolled out the dough, and then my grandmother, ever the artist, created cat-shaped cookies. She decorated one cookie as a Persian, and another as a Russian Blue, one had the markings of a Calico, and another the nub-like tale of a Manx.

J.P.

Grandma gave me a conspiratorial look as she sprinkled catnip on the one which resembled (but I didn't dare say it out loud) you know exactly who.

hen grandma removed the baking tray from the oven Rudolpha kept her distance. She feigned apathy but I'm sure she want- ed to know what was the business that we were about. The kettle started to squeal and Grandma poured tea for herself and for me. She lifted the cookies from the sheet but left one untouched for

special handling. I removed
the Tabby cookie and set it
down near my stocking foot.
I felt rubbing and purring as
Rudolpha found her treat.
We didn't offer our feast-
mate a cup of tea, but she
didn't seem to mind.

could see the snow falling fluffy fat as I looked out the kitchen window. I was trying to think courageous thoughts, trying to find a way to ask if I might take my sled down Northfield Hill even though it was one of Mom's "don'ts." So I sucked in a big breath of air and said "Granny I'll be really careful, and I won't go too fast, and I'll stay away from the pine stand, and I'll only stay out an hour, and I'll wear my red hat and . . ."

"Wendy," she said, "dress warmly, be careful, and really just for an hour." I thanked her and thanked her until she was pretty much pushing me out of the kitchen toward the hall closet door.

I remember my first run down Northfield Hill that day. The snow rushed by as the red blur that must have been me sledded down the hill. I took a smooth lean to the left to stay out of the pine stand and finished my run in triumph. I bounded back up the hill with my sled trailing behind me. I found my starting mark, counted

to three and . . . Somewhere between the second bump on Northfield Hill and the pine stand halfway down that slope an effervescent girl and an immovable object met with some force.

I awakened to the gentlest purring and big hazel eyes. I convalesced for several days, the victim of a bumped head, nasty scratches, and a bruised cheek that "will frighten your

mother something awful," Grandma said. Rudolpha lay, a guardian and ever vigilant, by day and by night on my bed. Mom and Dad returned on Christmas Eve as planned. I know I didn't look "as planned." After apologies and explanations, and Rudolpha looking at Mom with eyes that said "Wendy's all right, I looked after her like she was my

very own," everybody
remembered what day it was
and the spirit of the season
moved among us.

he following Thanksgiving Rudolpha took ill. Weeks of Grandma's ministering and numerous visits to the vet weren't enough to stop the inevitable. By the time we arrived at Grandma's for Christmas Rudolpha had passed away.

I knew, even though she
didn't want to sadden the day
by saying so, that Grandma
was thinking of her Rudolpha and was missing her.
I was gently touching the
ornaments Rudolpha had
always spied, poking at some
cat cookies Grandma had
baked, and looking at the
empty bay window, when
I began to sing:

On the first
day of Christmas
My Tabby
gave to me
A songbird in a
spruce tree.

On the second day of Christmas
My Persian gave to me
Two naughty mice
And a song bird in a spruce tree.

n the
third day of Christmas
My Calico gave to me
Three French rats
Two naughty mice
And a song bird
in a spruce tree.

*O*n the
fourth day of Christmas
My Short Hair gave to me
Four Puss 'n Boots
Three French rats
Two naughty mice
And a song bird in
a spruce tree.

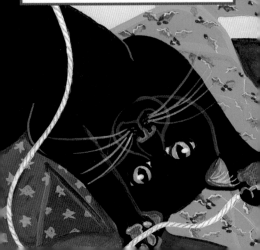

On the fifth day of Christmas
My Black Cat gave to me
Five yards of string
Four Puss 'n Boots
Three French rats
Two naughty mice
And a song bird in a spruce tree.

O n the

sixth day of Christmas

My Burmese gave to me

Six plants of catnip

Five yards of string

Four Puss 'n Boots

Three French rats

Two naughty mice

And a song bird in
a spruce tree.

*n the
seventh day of Christmas
My Siamese gave to me
Seven fish a-swimming
Six plants of catnip
Five yards of string
Four Puss 'n Boots
Three French rats
Two naughty mice
And a song bird in
a spruce tree.*

On the
eighth day of Christmas
My Manx gave to me
Eight fluffy catkins
Seven fish a-swimming
Six plants of catnip
Five yards of string
Four Puss 'n Boots
Three French rats
Two naughty mice
And a song bird in
a spruce tree.

On the ninth day
of Christmas
My Angora gave to me
Nine lizards leaping...

Eight fluffy catkins

~

Seven fish a-swimming

~

Six plants of catnip

~

Five yards of string

~

Four Puss 'n Boots

Three French rats

Two naughty mice

*And a song bird
in a spruce tree.*

n the
tenth day of Christmas
My Maine Coon gave to me
Ten luscious lobsters
Nine lizards leaping
Eight fluffy catkins
Seven fish a-swimming
Six plants of catnip
Five yards of string
Four Puss 'n Boots
Three French rats
Two naughty mice
And a song bird in
a spruce tree.

On the
eleventh day of Christmas
My Russian (Blue) gave to me
Eleven boots a stomping
Ten luscious lobsters
Nine lizards leaping
Eight fluffy catkins
Seven fish a-swimming
Six plants of catnip
Five yards of string
Four Puss 'n Boots
Three French rats
Two naughty mice
And a song bird in
a spruce tree.

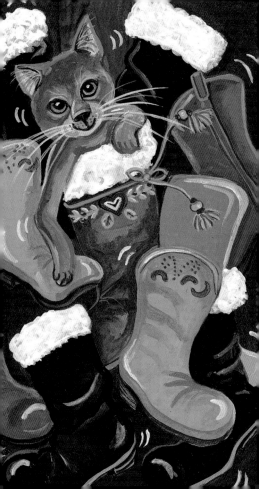

On the twelfth day
of Christmas
My kitten gave to me
Twelve pairs of mittens...

Eleven boots a stomping

Ten luscious lobsters

Nine lizards leaping

Eight fluffy catkins

Seven fish a-swimming

Six plants of catnip

Five yards of string

Four Puss 'n Boots

Three French rats

Two naughty mice

*And a song bird in
a spruce tree.*

When I finished the song, the look on Grandma's face made her appear as round and bright and jolly as I imagined Mrs. Claus to be when Santa returned home to her at the end of his globe-circling rounds. She hugged me with all the warmth and love that it is possible for a truly happy person to possess and gave me a sweet kiss on my forehead.

number of cats have come into my life since the day I first sang this song to Grandma.

I think fondly of them all, but none carries with him or her the holiday memories that I associate with Rudolpha. Each year before we prepare to enjoy our Christmas dinner we speak of how grateful we are for

life's bounty and the compa-
ny of our family and friends.
We sing *The 12 Cats of
Christmas*, inspired by the
joyous presence in our lives
that was for many years the
spirit of Christmas Cat.

THE END